Cyl

# The Ultimate Guide for How to Protect You and Your Children From A Cyber Bully

# Table Of Contents

# Introduction

This short book contains proven steps and strategies on how to protect yourself and your loved ones from cyberbullying. Perhaps you've already heard the names Hannah Smith, Sarah Lynn Butler, Jessica Logan, Tyler Clementi, Kenneth Weishuhn Jr., or Phoebe Prince. All of them committed suicide because of being the constant targets of cyberbullies.

In the hit TV musical series, *Glee,* the character Dave Karofsky attempted suicide after receiving hate messages and rude comments on his social media account for being gay. These are just a small sample of the many stories regarding cyberbullying, which have caught much attention because the victims were adolescents.

As one of the millions supporting the call for putting a stop to bullying and technology abuse, here is a book on how to protect yourself and your loved ones from cyberbullying. Everything you need to know about it is written in this short and concise guide, from getting to know cyberbullying from a legal perspective, what makes it different from other types of bullying, and family-friendly tips on how to avoid it.

You'll also get to know why kids are more prone to cyberbullying, and for parents, there is a quick guide on the things you should do when your child is the cyberbully. Also included are details of anti-cyberbullying campaigns around the world, as well as cyberbullying as depicted in popular culture.

Thanks again for grabbing this book. Hopefully you can get a few positive bits of information out of it!

# Chapter 1:

# An Overview on Cyberbullying

Cyberbullying can be defined as the use of the Internet and other related forms of technology to harass or harm people in a hostile, repeated, and deliberate manner.

As cyberbullying has become more common in our current society, awareness and legislation campaigns have intensified their efforts to curb it.

# Difference between Cyberbullying & Cyberstalking

Cyberbullying is not limited to children. While the behavior is often identified by the same characterization when practiced by teens and adults, the peculiarity in age groups sometimes refers to cyberbullying as a form of cyberstalking.

Some of the many common tactics cyberstalkers use are performed on social media, public forums, and online information sites. They do this to simply threaten an individual's safety, employment, earnings, and/or reputation. Such behaviors include encouraging other people to harass the victim's online activity, or worse, damage his/her reputation at school or at work.

Identity theft, monitoring in-depth online activity, creating false accusations, and damaging equipment or data are considered cyberstalking. Infiltrating confidential information about the individual and soliciting minors for sexual activities as a way of harassment is also considered both cyberstalking and cyberbullying. Unlike cyberbullying however, cyberstalking usually covers patterns of online and offline behavior.

# Legal Definition of Cyberbullying

In legal glossaries, cyberbullying is referred to as:

- Use of mobile technologies and internet service (i.e. forum discussion groups, web pages, social networking sites) with the intention to harm an individual or group.

- Use of communication technologies with the intention to harm an individual

- Technology-based actions using advanced communication and information technologies to support hostile, repeated, and deliberate behavior towards an individual or group as intention to harm, harass, or ruin positive character.

- Examples of actions that constitute cyberbullying include using technology to put down, manipulate, control, intimidate, humiliate, or falsely discredit a recipient.

The National Crime Prevention Council describes cyberbullying as "using the Internet, mobile phones and other devices to post and/or send text and images intended to embarrass a person, group, or organization."

# Cyberbullying Methods

As summarized by many anti-cyberbullying manuals:

Cyberbullying may be a case of someone pretending to be you online. When someone uses your name or photos and in any way pretends to be you, it means that he/she is bullying you. Why? Because the person is trying to conceal their own identity and aren't brave enough to stand by their own actions.

Cyberbullying is perpetrated through denigration, cyberstalking, harassment, impersonation and nasty exclusion of someone from an online group. This includes a person who spreads rumors and lies about you, it means that the said person is already cyberbullying you. Of course, when someone gossips about you and puts you in a negative light, it means that he/she is not trustworthy and that the person is out there to put you down. It's so easy to spread rumors online, so cyber-bullies think that they have the world in their hands. Some people are happy when they feel like they're better than others.

Cyberbullying involves repetitious behavior of harming a person's family. The thing with some people is that they pretend to be your friend. They pretend to be on your side and so when they get your trust and are able to make you spill your deepest, darkest secrets, it's easy for them to use those things against you. They can bully you by blackmailing you and saying that they will reveal your secrets if you will not do what they want. Some people also ask you to post nude or lewd photos or have "cyber-sex" with them just so they would not reveal your secrets. You probably know too well about how some celebrities get maligned when someone posts nude or discomforting photos and videos of them online. If it can happen to celebrities, it can happen to ordinary people, too.

Cyberbullying is as simple as sending text messages or emails harassing a person who doesn't want any contact with the sender. Cyberbullying may also include getting into public actions like sexual remarks, repeated threats, defamatory accusations, and "hate speeches." These days, it's so easy to harass someone by posting hurtful messages about them online. The most cowardly of individuals even do it anonymously because some websites allow users to be anonymous.

Cyberbullying is also done by asking others to gang up on someone. A cyberbully can convince anyone to target a person as a subject of ridicule in social networking sites and online forums. A cyberbully can also hack information or vandalize the person's website pages and post false statements.

Cyberbullying is limited to creating or posting gossip about a person online with the intent to convince others to direct their hate towards that person. It may reach the extent of identifying victims of online materials published to humiliate them.

Additionally, a cyberbully can disclose his/her target victim's personal info (i.e. full name, complete address, occupation, social security number, credit card information) in forums or websites wherein they can create fake accounts and write foul comments. This allows the cyberbully to hide his/her real identity, which makes it difficult for law enforcers to trace such activities.

# Children & Teens Involved in Cyberbullying

Based on research, boys initiate cyberbullying more often than girls do. In middle school, however, girls are found to be the ones that are more engaged in cyberbullying than boys. Whether the cyberbully is male or female, the main purpose of this nasty online behavior is to put up embarrassing statements against someone whom they envy.

In many junior high schools, cyberbullying occurs via blogs, email and text messaging. As the number of cyberbullies among the youth continues to increase, studies on the psycho-social effects of internet usage are being conducted. Experts begin to weigh in on the impact of cyberbullying, not just among victims, but also among the cyberbullies themselves.

Consequences of cyberbullying among children and teens are multi-faceted; it doesn't only affect their online behavior, but also their social life. Research on adolescent behavior reported that changes in a child or teen's behavior can be a result of cyberbullying. Victims, on the other hand, likely "create a cognitive pattern of bullies which helps them recognize people with aggressive behavior".

The Journal of Psychosocial Research on cyberbullying meanwhile reported that victims of cyberbullying are prone to disillusionment, loneliness, having low self-esteem, trust issues and, worse, suicide. Five out of ten teens that commit suicide do so after being involved in a bullying incident - a staggering number.

# Adults Involved In Cyberbullying

Just like physical bullying, cyberbullying has criminal consequences. From a target's level of understanding, cyberbullying is an extension of cyberstalking among many adults. Adult cyberbullies are usually motivated by pathological obsession, failure to fulfill a dream job, rejection, envy, and intention to intimidate others, only to make others feel inferior to them.

A cyberbully can be delusional; he/she wants to instill fear in someone to justify his/her online status. According to the British National Bullying Line Advice, most adult cyberbullies harass people as a way of dealing with their own inadequacies in life.

# Cyberbullying vs. Traditional Bullying

Several characteristics inherited from online activities can possibly raise the likelihood that people will exploit others for unusual purposes. Unlike traditional bullying, cyberbullying is done by anonymous individuals. Cyberbullies use pseudonyms, bogus email accounts and fake social media profiles to hide their real identities, which somewhat makes them free from social and normative restraints from their behavior.

The lack of Internet supervision is the reason why cyberbullying occurs. While many web chat hosts monitor the dialogue in chat rooms in an effort to trace offenders, private messages are only viewable between the sender and recipient.

Additionally, because teens are more aware of mobile phones and computers than adults are, they can engage in any mobile or internet activity without parental consent. Some teens are using this to their advantage to harass a person or group. Cyberbullying penetrates the walls of the home. In other words, many cyberbullies conduct their activity at home since no one will see them.

# Chapter 2:

# Protecting You And Yours

## Effects of Cyberbullying

Any form of bullying can make a person feel embarrassed, helpless, angry, isolated, and even suicidal. In most cyberbullying cases, a victim suffers from anxiety, depression, and low self-esteem. What's even worse is that cyberbullying can be more painful than physical bullying because:

It can happen anytime, anywhere. Even the safest places can be prone to cyberbullies/cyberbullying like the home, school, and workplace.

It can be witnessed by many people. Emails and text messages can be forwarded to hundreds or even thousands of people within seconds. Online comments and social media posts, meanwhile, can be seen by anyone. The farther reaching the cyberbullying, the more humiliation and paranoia the victim will feel.

Cyberbullying can be done anonymously, so you're not sure who is targeting you through gossip, hate messages and harassment, to name a few. Cyberbullying makes the victim feel more threatened since online anonymity simply means that posers are not that easy to identify.

# How to Know When Someone Is Being Cyber-Bullied

For the sake of this book, it's also important that you know how to read the signs that someone is already being cyber-bullied. This might even save a life, by allowing you to give help or make sure that a victim gets the help that he/she needs right away.

Certain things that you should be aware of include:

- When they suddenly start losing interest in using the computer or going online;

- When they do not want to talk about the internet or what they are doing with the computer;

- When they appear uncomfortable after receiving an instant message or an e-mail and when they don't feel like opening the message at all or proceed to delete it right away;

- When a person feels uneasy in social situations or when listening to you talk about the internet;

- When a person feels sad, angry, or agitated after using the computer;

- When a person becomes withdrawn and no longer seems to enjoy the things he/she used to enjoy doing.


Cyber-bullying can maim and kill, and in the next few chapters, you will learn what can be done          to          stop          it.

# Anti-Cyberbullying Tips for Kids & Teens

If you are targeted by a cyberbully, it's very important not to reply to any posts or messages written against you, no matter how insulting or hurtful those may be. Replying will only worsen the entire situation. Provoking a reaction from the victim, or anyone concerned, is what the cyberbully is looking for, so DO NOT give them the satisfaction they want.

It's also very important not to get revenge by being a cyberbully back to them. Again, it will only worsen the situation and can lead to criminal charges being filed against you. Instead, respond towards cyberbullying by:

Being relentless. Cyberbullying is barely limited to two or three incidents. This means it often appears as a sustained attack against someone for an extended period of time. Just like a cyberbully, the victim can be relentless by reporting every single incident related to cyberbullying. The flip side of the wide reach of the online platforms is that you can report users, whether it be through YouTube, Twitter, Facebook, etc. Websites that have a large reach also usually have a process in which you can report abuse fairly effectively.

Report threats of inappropriate sexual messages or harm to the authorities. In most cases, the cyberbully's actions are prosecutable by law.

Block the cyberbully's email address, mobile number, and social media contacts. You can report the cyberbully's activities via the websites or the internet service providers they use in targeting victims.

Save any evidence of cyberbullying. For example, take a screenshot of a webpage or save text messages before reporting them to your parents, friends, teachers, web administrators, or the police.

## If you are cyberbullied:

Never blame yourself. It's not your fault that you are being cyberbullied. No matter what the cyberbully does or says, you shouldn't feel embarrassed about yourself or your feelings towards other people. Remember, it's the cyberbully who's almost always having the biggest internal problems, not you.

Never beat yourself up. Do not make a particular case of cyberbullying worse by dwelling on it (e.g. reading all the hate messages over and over again). Instead, DELETE (after saving and storing it) any cyberbullying-related messages on your personal accounts and focus on cherishing positive experiences.

Try to see cyberbullying from a different perspective. Think about the cyberbully as someone who is just a person desperate enough to go to these lengths. Also think about the cyberbully as a frustrated person who wants to take control of your feelings. Do not let him or her control your feelings but try to understand their motives nonetheless.

Learn to deal with depression, anxiety, or stress. Finding ways to relieve these feelings makes you more resilient so that you won't get overwhelmed and lash out towards others.

Seek help from a friend, teacher, or any trusted adult. Seeking help from a counselor doesn't hurt either; they deal with cyberbullying cases fairly often and will be able to help you without making you feel embarrassed.

Spend a lot of quality time doing stuff that you enjoy. The more time you spend doing stress-free activities like playing any kind of sport or going on a trip outdoors, the less significance cyberbullying will have on you. It is when you are coped up in front of your computer that your mind begins to scramble for all the worse-case scenarios.

# Anti-Cyberbullying Tips for Parents

No matter how painful it is, some kids are reluctant to tell their parents or teachers about cyberbullying. This is often times because kids believe that telling these adults may result in them getting grounded or punished — no mobile phones, video games, watching TV, etc.

While it is the parents' responsibility to monitor their children's use of technology, especially the Internet, it's very important not to threaten or punish them just because they are bullied.

For parents, your child may be a victim of cyberbullying if he/she:

Shows changes in appetite, sleep, behavior, mood, anxiety, or signs of depression.

Avoids participation in group activities and even refuses to go to school.

Keeps getting poor grades in school even while showing desire at home.

Withdraws from family, friends, or activities that were joyful in the past.

Is secretive about his/her internet activities and/or avoids discussions about the Internet.

Becomes visibly anxious whenever he or she receives a text message or an email.

Becomes visibly distressed, angry, or sad after using a mobile phone or a computer.

# Protecting Children from Cyberbullying

To ensure that your children are as safe as possible when they go online, teach them how to:

Always show politeness online, just like how they should behave in real life.

Not send messages when angry, stressed, or upsct.

Not put anything online that will cause humiliation among their friends and classmates.

Not talk about gossip or the lives of others.

Never share their internet passwords with anyone outside of the family.

Never share or post their personal information (full name, home address, parents' names, credit card numbers, social security numbers, etc.) or their friends' own.

Delete cyberbullying-related messages and block cyberbullies on their social media accounts (if they have any).

# Monitoring Children's Internet Use

Regardless of how much your child will resent it, you can only protect him/her by monitoring his or her online activities.

Here are some tips:

Limit data access on your child's mobile phone if he/she is using it to surf the internet. Some wireless internet providers allow mobile users to turn off messaging services anytime of the day.

Place the computer in the busiest area of your house. This way, you can easily monitor it when it is being used by your child. If he/she is using a laptop or a smartphone, you can also do the same.

Always know who your child is communicating with online. Go over his/her online address book (i.e. his/her "buddy list" on IM or friends list on Facebook). Ask who each person is and how he/she knows your child.

# Chapter 3:

# What To Do If...

Hearing about children becoming victims of cyberbullying is heartbreaking for parents, but what if their child is the cyberbully? It will definitely trigger shock and worry amongst parents. The very first response to this problem is usually disbelief. How could your child be capable of hurting others? Recognizing how easy it is for children to cyberbully keeps parents from overreacting.

Some parents are often caught off-guard upon learning about their child's nasty online behavior because they have probably heard of cyberbullying cases from school or from parents of cyberbully victims. However, this isn't an excuse to freak out or even to beat yourself up for being a bad parent.

Follow the ideas explained below and address your child's cyberbullying in a calm, sensible manner.

# Listen

Listening to your child may sound easy, but if you are contacted by another person (i.e., a teacher or guidance counselor) regarding your child's bad deeds, it can be difficult. You'll likely experience a range of emotions and your initial reaction will be to defend your child.

Instead, do your best to stay calm and quiet. Listen to every detail and, if possible, ask for copies of referenced correspondence from the people who first noticed your child's cyberbullying. This way, it will be much easier for you to address your child in person.

# Talk To Your Child

Tell your child what others have told you regarding his/her online behavior. If possible, show your child proof of a cyberbullying incident he/she was a part of. Allow him/her to explain his/her side of the incident without interruptions in between.

Your goal here is to acknowledge what your child has done and to make him or her accept responsibility for the action.

# Accept Your Child's Problem

While it is not a good idea to assume that your child is guilty of cyberbullying without letting him/her explain first, it is very important to accept the gravity of his/her situation.

Seek help from a teacher or professional that can speak to your child about cyberbullying. Express your concerns and commit yourself to dealing with your child's situation.

Expect the child to try and rationalize the bullying going on, as he/she does not want to look like a bad person in your eyes, but remember to stay grounded and go by the facts.

# Accept That Your Child Made A Mistake

Accepting your child's mistakes (not just cyberbullying) and taking action is important. It is your responsibility to respond to his/her cyberbullying issues appropriately and prevent related incidents from happening again in the future.

Denying or ignoring your child's behavior will only worsen the problem; it will only cause him/her to keep on harassing other people.

# Support Your Child's School Activities

If the school implements a strict rule prohibiting any form of bullying or cyberbullying, support it. As challenging as it may be for some, supporting your child's school activities is your way of telling him/her that any form of bullying is unacceptable and should not be tolerated.

Having a support system is one of the best ways of ensuring your child won't bully or cyberbully others again.

# Implement Some Consequences

After cyberbullying has occurred, allow your child to learn how to handle proper online communication. The best way you can do this is by taking away his/her computer or mobile phone for a while. Before doing this, however, you need to explain your reasons clearly to your child. Otherwise, he/she might get angry or fight back.

Let your child understand the importance of online etiquette, not only in dealing with others, but also with themselves. Once your child has already stopped cyberbullying or demonstrating any nasty behavior online, you can give back his/her gadgets. As a side note, some social networking sites have a "Parental Control" feature that allows parents to see what their children are posting.

# Be Aware of Legal Issues Concerning Cyberbullying

In the United States of America, the punishment for cyberbullying varies by state. That being said, it is necessary to research your state's policy on cyberbullying. Determine how the chosen state handles cyberbullying incidents among teenagers.

Some state laws have included "sexting" as one of the many provisions of cyberbullying. So if you live in New York and you're using sexually suggestive messages to bully a person, you can be charged with cyberbullying.

# Understanding the Consequences

Many children believe that online statements aren't recognized by the law. Thus, they make this an excuse to cyberbully people. As a result, they tend to underestimate their online reputation.

In a world where technology and social media is becoming more and more transparent, this can come back to haunt them later on in their lives. Make sure to give them this perspective as well.

It is the parents' responsibility to help their children understand the consequences whenever they harass someone. There are so many possible consequences, none of them pleasant. Just read the stories about Phoebe Prince, Amanda Todd, and Jessica Logan.

Here, your goal is to show to your child how cyberbullying can hurt others, even long after the actual incident of bullying.

# Increase Knowledge on the Internet

Don't let the World Wide Web keep you away from learning. You don't necessarily have to keep pace with your child every minute, but you should at least stay informed with what he/she is doing whenever he/she sits at the computer. It's important to find a trusted resource for information regarding anything you need to learn about the Internet, especially social networking.

There are many things you can try so that bullies do not ruin your child's life, whether online or not. You don't need to give them a space in your life because they do not deserve to be there. You should keep the evidences, yes, but you have all the right not to reply to them, because doing so would only make them feel like they are in control of your life now.

Aside from not replying to them, it would also be good for you to block those bullies. The bullies may think that you're just being a coward but the truth is that blocking them means that you care about yourself and that you care about your safety. There are various ways of blocking people on various websites and there are also guidelines as to how or why you can report them to the administrators of the websites. Here's what you have to keep in mind:

## Youtube

Youtube has a safety center where you can report anything, from a person's abusive comments or messages, to videos that contain self-harming, harassment, and bullying of any kind. Just check out youtube.com/yt/policyandsafety and let your voice be heard.

## Vine

When it comes to this micro-video sharing site, you can report someone who uses an unauthorized trademark, impersonates you, or posts sexually explicit or pornographic content.

## Twitter

You can block someone by going to their profile and clicking on "block". Meanwhile, you can report a user if he/she is impersonating you or someone you know, using unauthorized trademarks, posting links with regards to your private information, or threatening or abusing you in any way.

## Tumblr

With Tumblr, you can block someone by going to this person's profile and clicking on "block". They also have a report to Tumblr via e-mail policy. To do this, just use the word "harassment" in the subject line and in the body of your e-mail - together with your report, attach a screengrab/photo of the hateful message/photos/videos and add the details of the Tumblr user who is harassing you in the e-mail. Make sure that you give as much detail as possible so necessary actions can be taken right away. Send the report to support@tumblr.com.

## Instagram

You can check out Instagram's Safety Center to report someone who is impersonating, hacking, exposing private information, sexually threatening, or exploiting you in any possible way.

## Facebook

You can report someone if he/she posts pictures of self-harming, abusing people/animals, posting violent and nasty threats/messages - whether on your wall or through the inbox, posting hateful messages against one's sexual orientation, race, gender, medical condition, disability, posting nudity or graphic content, and spamming. Just click on the "report now" button or click "block" on the person's name so he/she no longer has access to you.

## Ask.fm

This is one of those sites that allows users to be anonymous and that's also the reason why there are a lot of cyberbullying victims who experienced bullying from the members of this site. Even if that's the case though, you can easily report people, even if you are not logged in. To do this, just move the cursor down someone's profile.

After doing so, you will see an option whether to like the post or report it as abusive. You can do so if the message/user is spamming, posting hate/violent speech or photos accompanying their posts, and posting pornographic content. If you are using the ask.fm app through Facebook or Twitter, you can also just click on it and choose to "report/contact this app" to report your situation.

Now that you know what to do with bullies on each of these websites, it will be easier for you to deal with them and to help others out as well.

# Ensure That Your Child Is Taking Responsibility

As you explain to your child the consequences of being a cyberbully, you can't help but sometimes worry that he/she is not sincere in listening to you. All forms of bullying inflict pain and humiliation, and dealing with it is not easy for the victims.

Make sure that your child will take note of his/her responsibility in taking the necessary actions to avoid cyberbullying others. As much as possible, write down notes and paste them in your child's room.

You can also be more responsible by reminding your child of the following:

## Don't share your passwords with others

It's so hard to trust people when it comes to your online accounts. It's always safer to just keep the passwords to yourself and to know that you're the only one who has access to your private details such as information and photos or videos. Secrets are meant to be kept and not spilt.

## Don't send messages when you're upset or angry.

This can trigger reactions from different kinds of people and may even provoke people to say nasty things against you. If you feel like lashing out via technology, take a deep breath and think about all the positive things in your life. If possible, sleep on the thought and get in a workout the following morning - after all that, see if you still want to respond in the same manner.

**Don't put anything online that you would not want other people to see.**

Don't post photos that have you in uncompromising positions—even privately. Hackers can always check your account. It's important that you protect yourself by maintaining your privacy.

Remember that even if you delete something from your account, search engines can keep them so they'll forever be on the internet. In other words, be smart and vigilant—especially when it comes to things regarding your privacy.

**You can set limits for your child's internet usage**

You can choose not to give them gadgets first, unless they are done with something you asked them to do, or unless you have educated them about the risks. You can also limit the time of their internet usage or choose to put the computer in the living room, especially if the child is pretty young so you can monitor how he/she uses it.

Make sure not to pry too much though and just be a friend to your child. Make him/her understand that you know they need the internet but that you also want to make him/her feel safe and that if anything happens, they can talk to you about it.

## Set ground rules

These ground rules should not just be about the internet but about your child's behavior, in general. It's important for parents to raise their children in a manner wherein even if the kids see them as friends, they never disregard the fact that the parents are still their parents and that they are supposed to be respected.

If you learn how to treat kids this way, it will become easier for them to understand that they won't get what they want all the time and that sometimes, they just have to deal with it and not hurt others in the process. Make them realize that bravery is not about belittling others, but rather, knowing how to deal with the life that was given to you and learning how to make the most out of it.

## Always Remember: There Are TWO SIDES to Every Story

While letting your child admit that he/she cyberbullied a fellow child can be quite challenging, keep in mind that it's a natural thing for children to control their behavior. In some cases, cyberbullies can manipulate the incident before the parent or entire school finds out. With these instances, it's very important to also take the side of the victim without judging.

# Chapter 4:

# Save Evidence and Report the Case

You can report whatever it is that happened to you. Just because you were bullied online doesn't mean that it's any less than being bullied physically or personally.

The first thing you have to keep in mind is that you have to save the evidence of bullying. Why? Because without this, it may be hard to reprimand those cyber-bullies and it will be much harder to track them down.

It is also important to remember that even if someone posted anonymously, you don't have to feel like the case is a dead end because investigators can track IP addresses.

**Keep screenshots of text/instant messages,** e-mails, anonymous messages, and the website on which your online account is on, so that you have the evidence with you. And then report the incident to your parents, guardians, or school counselors. There are also websites and hotlines where you can report cases of cyberbullying. Some of which include:

## The Police

When things are getting out of hand, you can definitely tell the police about it. Do this when your privacy is being threatened, when someone asks you to post lewd photos/videos, when someone posts lewd photos/videos of you or of him/herself and forcing you to do the same, or when you are being stalked or threatened in any way.

**The Office for Civil Rights or the Civil Rights Division of the Department of Justice**, if you are being bullied because of your race, color, religion, sexual orientation, or disability.

**The National Suicide Prevention Hotline (1-800-273-TALK)**, if you/someone you know is already feeling helpless about your situation and where counselors can talk to you and help you make sense of the situation.

**Cyberbullyhotline.com,** where not only can you report what's going on with you but where you can also see infographics about the state of bullying in your hometown or in different parts of the country.

**A guidance counselor or a teacher**.

If you know the person who cyber-bullies you and if he/she attends the same school or work that you do, you can definitely tell a teacher, counselor, or employer about it. If that official still does not do anything, then it may be time for you to switch schools and/or tell the police.

If you're more comfortable talking to people your age, especially those who are also experiencing the same things that you are experiencing, you can try these hotlines and websites below:

1-877-OUT-IS-OK (For Residents of Canada)

1-866-4-U-TREVOR (For U.S. Residents)

1800-184-527 (For Residents of Australia)

0207-837-7324 (For U.K. Residents)

(04) 473-7858 (For Residents of New Zealand)

**Your-confessions.tumblr.com**, where you can post your confessions about being cyber-bullied or anything that plagues you down, as well as where you get access to a forum where you can share your experiences with other people and learn from those who have survived cyberbullying in the past.

**Beatbullying.org**, where you can chat with people who are going through the same things that you are going through in real time, and where you can join various causes and seek advice from counselors and professionals.

**Therearenouglyducklings.tumblr.com/submit,** where you can submit artwork, poems, essays or anything else about your situation that could help others out.

Remember, by speaking out, you are able to save yourself and save others one step at a time. If you don't start speaking out about your situation, you are only allowing bullies to take over your life—and that's not best for anyone!

# Chapter 5

# Disconnect and Unplug!

Sometimes, people get so addicted to the internet that they forget that they used to know how to live without it. Even though the internet is considered a necessity in the business world and school these days, remember that societies once thrived and functioned smoothly without it.

It's okay to deactivate your online accounts for a week or more and come back when you're ready. It's okay to appreciate life for what it is and to see that you can manage without the internet. You may think that it's impossible to take a break from the internet but you'll never know how life can be good without it unless you try. If you think you'll get bored, then try these activities below and you'll realize that life is fun without the internet. This may also shake up your online routines and tendencies, by forcing you out of your comfort zone!

## Write

Write in a journal, doodle away and just express your inner thoughts. By writing, you are able to exercise your demons and make yourself realize that you can let go of the things that weigh you down. It's also a good practice for school or work, by opening a channel of creativity.

## Watch a movie

You can get lost in the movie and have some cathartic moments. Sometimes, a good cry can help you. Or, watch any genre or re-watch some of your favorite films from years back.

## Walk around

Feel the air around you and stop and smell the roses. Sure, it's a cliché but sometimes, by walking around, you get to clear your mind and make yourself ready for the big things that are coming your way.

## Visit a park or an animal sanctuary

It can be quite rejuvenating to visit a park, an animal sanctuary, or any place where you can be surrounded by beautiful sceneries and creatures such as a butterfly gardens, a zoo, and the like.

## Travel!

Traveling is fun. You don't need to visit the most expensive destinations on earth—you can start with your own city or town and its hidden gems, then move on from there. What matters is that you get to realize that the world is so much more than just the four corners of your room. By learning about people's cultures and histories, you are able to learn more about yourself and the world in general.

## Spend time with family and friends

Don't get so caught up in the internet that you forget about the real people and relationships in your life. Spend some time with the people who matter.

## Sing!

Singing is a good way to release stress—plus, who knows? Maybe you could become the next singing sensation, or just let your silly side out!

## Read a book

The art of reading should not be lost. It can always be good to buy an actual, physical book instead of just downloading from the internet. It's also nice to get lost in books because it will make you learn a lot about various aspects and views of life, letting you realize that there's so much that you can learn about while you are living on this planet!

## Play video games

Use the Playstation or X-box or even your good old Nintendo, if you still have it with you. It's a good way to release some adrenaline.

## Play Solitaire

It's old-school, sure, but it'll always be fun!

## Play board games

It's a fun way to reminisce and have pure, uninterrupted fun.

## Go swimming

It's a form of exercise and it's relaxing and refreshing—literally and figuratively. Once you're in the water, you can easily feel relaxed and forget about your problems of the real world for a bit.

## Go on an adventure!

Try zip-lining, sky diving, bungee jumping, white water rafting—any adventure that you can think of. It's going to be fun and it'll surely be an experience that you won't forget.

## Go on a picnic

Bring your family, friends, or special someone with you. Or, you can even go on a picnic by yourself. Bring a book, some food, good music, and just revel in your solitude and serenity.

## Go get crafting!

It's always fun to make crafts because it's a good way to pass time and to release your creative juices. You can draw, paint, or do any kind of art you fancy.

## Go biking

It's never too late to learn how to ride a bicycle. It's one of the most useful things that you can learn in life because you can use a bike to go to the destination of your choice and it's also a good form of exercise.

## Get involved in a cause

Join a cause that speaks to you—such as anti-cyberbullying, animal rights, human rights—anything. It's good to be with people who share your passions and whom you can do beneficial and productive things with. It's always fun to help people and make a difference in their lives.

## Focus on what you need to do

If you're a student, focus on your studies. If you have a job, make sure that you do your best and make the most out of it. By learning how to channel your frustrations from your personal life into the ventures that you are involved in, you'll be able to create more influential, positive work. You can use the feelings you feel from bullying as fuel to build or accomplish something.

## Do some gardening

For many people, it's very therapeutic to just plant some flowers and trees and feel one with nature.

## Clean your room

You probably spend lots of time in your room alone with your thoughts, so it's just right that you keep it tidy and organized. Change your sheets, pillowcases and maybe even do a little room make-over by painting the walls or putting up some interesting wallpaper.

You can also rearrange things in your closet or drawers. It's time to throw the unnecessary items away and make room only for what you need and for better things to come. In a way, it's also symbolic of how you should only make room for the important things in life in your life.

## Binge-watch television shows

A good TV binge can always be therapeutic! Nothing beats the feeling of getting lost in a television show and just watching each and every episode, as you follow along the storyline.

# Chapter 6:

## Build Confidence

One of the most important things that you should keep in mind when it comes to dealing with bullies is that you should build your self-confidence.

You are doing this because someone who is confident is someone who can get more opportunities in life and is someone who can be happy without listening to the rants and comments of others. It's all about making yourself better, because you deserve only the best in life.

Here are a few helpful things you can do to build your confidence level:

## Spend some time getting to know yourself

Some may think that this is unnecessary or a waste of time, but the truth is if you know who you are and what it is that you want in life, then people will have a hard time bringing you down.

You won't be confused, more often than not, and you will not feel like the world is conspiring against you. If you know who you are, it will be hard for you to be affected by the things people say, think, and act around you.

## Speak Up

There's no use in trying to bottle your feelings. If you learn how to open up then the world will open up to you, and you won't have a hard time cruising through life. Speak up and let people see that you're a smart and thoughtful individual.

## Proper Grooming

Face it: When you look good then you feel good. It's all about knowing how to be prim and proper and knowing how to enjoy a good bath. Plus, it's always fun to get a hair cut, or change your hairstyle in anyway. The bottom line is that you have to help yourself look good, not for others, but for yourself.

## Have fun dressing up

Buy a new set of clothes or re-construct some of your old ones to turn them into something completely new. What matters is that you have fun dressing up because once you do, you'll be able to feel better about yourself. It's true that you can make-over yourself even if you are the weirdest, nerdiest, and most non-savvy person you know.

## Exercise

Not only will exercising make your body firmer and more beautiful, your health will also be in tip-top shape. If you are at the peak of health, you will be able to embark on a lot of adventures and opportunities, plus your happy hormones (endorphins) will also be released, so the aura of positivity fill your mind!

## Do what you love, love what you do

Sometimes, when people are doing things that they are not sure of or are not confident about, they feel like they are not able to do their job well and that they're supposed to find another job.

But, if you love what you're doing or if you have ways to release pain and angst by means of writing, art, doing crafts and the like, you'll see that everyone plays a significant role in the world and that it's important to love what you do and do what you love because it's so hard to live life feeling like you're not doing something worthwhile.

## Create positive vibes

You can do this by basking in a mantra every day. Upon waking up, look at yourself in the mirror and instead of saying *"Dang, you're so ugly"* or *"Why am I even living?"*, say *"I'm beautiful"* or *"Today's going to be awesome"* or *"I'm at Peace"*. Once you do this, you'll notice that you'll have a positive vibe and outlook all throughout the day.

This method is definitely so much better than feeling bad about yourself and whatever's going on around you. When you create positive vibes, you're able to show yourself that you are capable of doing a lot of things and that great things can happen for you. Say "*You Can*" instead of "*You Can't*" and you certainly will be able to do what you have to do throughout the day.

## Develop good posture

Stand tall and don't slump your shoulders. Walk with confidence and learn to face the day happily. If you have strong, confident posture, it will reflect even in pictures, and people will look up to you and see that you're a person who's hopeful and has a lot of potential within them.

## Be thankful for what you have

Most of the time, if you don't know how to be thankful for the things that you have in life, it's hard to see that life can bring forth a lot of great and amazing things. But, if you have an attitude of gratitude, even for the smallest things, it will be easy for you to attract more good things. One has to learn to be thankful because it makes life so much lighter and better.

Remember, by building confidence, you are able to arm yourself against people who could bring you down. Instead of letting these people bring you down, pick yourself up and know that you can do great things on your own—but you have to believe in yourself first.

# Chapter 7

# Other Things You Need to Know

## Cyberbullying Awareness Campaigns

### United States

In March of 2007, the American Advertising Council, the Crime Prevention Coalition of America, the Department of Justice, and the National Crime Prevention Council all joined forces in an effort to raise awareness about cyberbullying by launching a public service campaign to educate teens on how to put a stop to cyberbullying. In a survey conducted among teenagers by American Life and PEW Internet, 40% of the respondents claimed that they were victims of cyberbullying at least once in their life.

In January of 2008, the Boy Scouts of America added in their handbook the basics of dealing with cyberbullies. This was in response to reported cases of cyberbullying between its members. Not long afterwards, FOX 11 News featured a report on cyberbullying and other cruel online activities done by organizations like STICKAM, who initially used the codename "Brothas" in infiltrating private accounts of some famous personalities.

In June of 2008, teachers, parents, students and internet experts gathered in White Plains, New York City for a 2-day event called *Wired Safety's International Anti-Cyberbullying Conference.* Executives from various internet portals and social networking sites talked in front of thousands about methods on how to protect their businesses, careers, and character reputations from cyberbullying.

The event was sponsored by top companies such as AOL, McAfee, Microsoft, Disney, KidZui, Procter & Gamble, US Children Safety Research Center, and Verizon. These companies are also recognized for their anti-cyberbullying advocacies.

## Spain

In Spanish communities, there are many non-profit organizations supporting methods in putting a stop to cyberbullying. These organizations report any case of cyberbullying to police, provide massive awareness campaigns, and talk to victims.

Among some NGOs active in promoting anti-cyberbullying in the country are Agencia Espanola De Proteccion de Datos, Actua Contra el Ciberacoso, Spanish Association of Internet Users, Pantallas Amigas, and Spanish Association of Parents and Children.

## Australia

The Australian Covert Cyberbullying Prevalence Survey took part in the nationwide assessment of cyberbullying experiences among nearly 8,000 teens. According to Australian Covert, cyberbullying incidences in the country have increased by 10% since 2009.

# Preventive Legislation on Cyberbullying

Many researchers suggest that anti-cyberbullying programs must be implemented in ALL schools. Administrators can incorporate these programs into the school curriculum. As of 2011, there are 50 North American institutions providing lessons on internet privacy and online safety.

If all schools implemented this, parents would have more reasons to teach their children proper ways of protecting themselves from cyberbullying and using the Internet in general.

# Pop Culture's Role in Anti-Cyberbullying

Movies and television programs continue to play a crucial role in presenting the effects of cyberbullying among teens. As mentioned earlier, the musical TV show, *Glee*, once featured an episode on cyberbullying. Movies like *Odd Girl Out*, *Adina's Deck*, *At a Distance* and *Cyberbully* tackle modern-day issues regarding cyber crimes.

In J.K. Rowling's adult contemporary novel *The Casual Vacancy*, one of the protagonists became a subject of embarrassing images posted on Facebook. Documentaries of cyberbullying victims are currently being aired on various TV networks as well.

# Conclusion

Hopefully this short, concise book was able to help you and your loved ones protect yourselves from cyberbullying.

The next step is to share your experiences as your way of encouraging people, especially young ones, to project a decent online image by not posting hurtful, insulting, degrading, and/or humiliating messages against a person or group.

Thank you and good luck implementing this information!

42124653R00044

Made in the USA
Middletown, DE
01 April 2017